RUBY
and the
DRAGON

Gareth Owen
illustrated by
Bob Wilson

PictureLions

An Imprint of HarperCollinsPublishers

We're going to
do something
special today.

Class 4 was in school.

Miss Williams said,

She brought out a big box.

Everyone wondered what was in the box.

Is it a doll?
Is it a football?
Is it a pork-pie?
Is everybody here?

Please, Miss.

Ruby was late.

We can't open the box
until Ruby is here.

Ruby was always late for school.

She saw the poster on the wall.

Ruby liked animals.

COME TO IPSTONES ZOO
IT'S GRREAT

I'd like to be a parrot or a polar bear, or best of all I'd like to be a....

The crossing lady said,

Shouldn't you be in school?

ARRRGH!
I'm a crocodile,

replied Ruby.

Ruby walked into the playground.

Arrgh..

Arrgh...

Grrgh!!

Good morning.
I'm a crocodile.

GRRGH!!
Very nice, Ruby.
Sit down now.

We're going to
open the box.

Please Miss,
What's in the box?
A cake?
A puppy?
A ghost!?

In the box there
is a dress...
and a helmet...

AND....

WILLIAM
DREW THIS

A DRAGON!

It's not a real dragon.
It's a make-believe dragon.
These are all costumes.
Costumes for a play.
Now, who knows what a play is?
Miss. Miss. Me, Miss!
A play is when you pretend.
Good girl, Ruby.
We are going to do a play.
Everybody will come to see it.
Now, who shall we have to play the princess?
The princess wears a beautiful dress.
Miss. Miss. Me. Miss!

Ruby tried on the dress.

What do you think?

FISH SWIM
BIRDS FLY
HORSES RUN
A FISH BY RUBY
Very nice, Ruby.
Angela, you try the dress on.

Angela tried on the dress.

!?

It fitted her perfectly.

I am princess Angela.
I never really wanted to be princess, anyway.

You have to be soppy to be princess.
That will do, Ruby.

Now the prince.
The prince wears a helmet
and carries a sword.
He is very strong and brave.

Who shall we have
to play the prince?

FOOD EAT

Miss. Miss,
Me. Miss !!

How does
it look?

Raymond, you try
the helmet on.

am prince
aymond.

I never really
wanted to be
prince, anyway.

You have to have a
big head to be prince.

That's
enough!

Ruby tried on the helmet.

Next we have - the dragon. Prince Raymond kills the dragon. The dragon costume fits over your head; nobody will see you.
Who would like to play the dragon?
The dragon has a loud voice. Is there anyone in the class with a loud voice?
Miss Williams said,
Ruby. You will play the dragon.

Ruby didn't want to be the dragon.

Nobody will see me inside the dragon.
The Princess wears a beautiful dress.
The Prince has a helmet and a sword.
The dragon gets killed by the Prince!!
Please Miss, I don't want to be dragon.
Don't be silly, Ruby.
Arrgh..
Arrrgh..
It's a very ugly dragon.
GRRGH!!
I always wanted to be the dragon.

Ruby tried on the dragon costume.

It fitted perfectly.

She looked fierce.

She felt fierce.

Raymond said,

Ruby said,

Ruby wore her costume every day.

She wore it at mealtimes.

Sorry Mum. Dragons don't eat cabbage.

She wore it in the street.

Arrgh...

Arrgh...

GRRRH!

The postman was surprised.

Arrgh..

And in the garden.

GRRH!

The cat was surprised.

The award for best actress in the universe goes to Ruby Turner for her part as the dragon.

She wore it in bed.

The school was empty.

They're all in the hall.

They peeped through the door.

I am Raymond, Prince of Ipstones.

The two men crept towards the headmaster's office.

Mr Jones did not wake up.

It's your turn soon, Ruby,
PAINT STORE

said Miss Williams.

When you hear your line turn left outside the door, then turn right and you'll be on the stage. Make sure you come on stage at the right time, and let the Prince win.

Arrgh-grrhh,

said Ruby.

She heard her line.

I hope the **dragon** isn't nearby.
PAINT STORE

She practised swinging her head like a dragon.

Aaaah.

She knocked down a tin of powder paint.
The powder went up her nose.

She sneezed.
CHOO!
The head fell over her eyes; she couldn't see.
Where was the door?
This feels like the handle of a door.
PAINT STORE
It was the wrong door.
POST OFFICE RED
DONE UP YELLOW
WAZ PAINT

She found the right door.

Ruby was not very good at directions,

or at remembering things.

Now, was it left and then right?
or was it right and then right?
or left, right, and then left?
or right, left and left right!?
Now I remember! Miss Williams said - right and then left.

At school they practised every day.

ARRGH.GRRH!!
Is that a dragon I hear?

Raymond was the prince. He fought the dragon with his sword.

Fear not Princess..
I will kill the dragon.
Arrgh..

Ruby. You have to let the Prince win.

ARREOWH!!! OH! OH! AH! eeee gurgle
!?
Was that better?
Very nice, Ruby.

The day of the play came round.   Everybody was in the hall.

The headmaster was there.   The Mayor was there.

Ruby's mummy and daddy were there.

Ruby was nervous.

Angela was nervous.

Raymond was nervous

In the dressing room Ruby practised her lines.

RUBY'S
LINES
GRR
ARGH!
ARRGRR
GRR GRR
ARGH!
GRRR
ARGH!
AR
GRR
AR
GRRH!!

Miss Williams looked in.

We're ready to
start the play.

Miss Williams made a speech.

Welcome to St George's School.
Our play is called - 'The Prince,
the Princess, and the dragon.'
I hope you will enjoy it.

Everybody clapped.

The school was empty; everybody was at the play.

The money was on the headmaster's desk.

The cups were on the shelf.

Mr Jones was asleep.

Two men climbed in through the window.

We'll steal the money and the cups.
SWAG

They were burglars.

She went down the wrong corridor.

She turned left.

THIS WAY
TO THE PLAY

On the stage Angela said,

Prince Raymond, listen
I think I can hear the
dragon coming this way.

But she was wrong.

The dragon was lost.

Mr Jones was asleep.   The two burglars were hard at work.

That's all the money.
Now for those cups.
HEADMASTER

Everybody was waiting for Ruby.

Oh no! I think I can see the dragon.

Miss Williams went to the dressing room.

We're waiting for you, Ruby.

Are you in the cupboard?

Ruby wasn't in the cupboard.

Ruby was outside the staff-room door.

DRAGON!?

So I said to her – Doreen, that dress is far too long. It'll drag on the floor.

She took a deep breath, and burst through the door.

Arrrgh...Arrgh. GRRRHH!!
Eeeek! It's a dragon!

It was the wrong door.

Everybody was still waiting for Ruby.

I said.....OH NO!.. I CAN SEE THE DRAGON!
I can't.
Nor me.
It must be a very small dragon.

Miss Williams was following the dragon's footprints.

Ruby. Ruby! Where are you!?

Ruby was outside the headmaster's door.

These cups are priceless.
HEADMAN

PRINCESS!?

She took a big breath...

Aarrgh..

...and burst through the door.
GRRRH!
It's a...d.; dd..dragon!
Mr Jones woke up.
HELP! HELP!
Raymond, come back! Why are you running away!?
We're being chased by a DRAGON!

The burglars ran off down the corridor.   Ruby ran after them.

TO THE PLAY
Raymond.
Come back!

Mr Jones went into the headmaster's office.

XMAS
CONCERT
FUNDS

The money!

The cups!

Miss Williams arrived.

What's
happened?
I dreamed that
I heard a dragon.
HEADMASTER
Which way
did it go?

Miss Williams ran off down the corridor.

Ruby. Come back!

Mr Jones rang the police.

St George's school. Come quickly!
We've been burgled.
A cat-burglar, do you think?
No. More like a dragon-burglar

Everybody was *still* waiting for the dragon.

Why is nothing happening?
Where can the dragon be?
Come on, Ruby.

If she doesn't come soon.. I'll kill her.

Then, at last,
they heard footsteps.
They were coming towards
the stage.
And so, in a very loud voice,
Angela cried out...

and Miss Williams ran onto the stage.

Prince Raymond, look. It's the hideous dragon.
Excuse me. Has anyone seen Ruby?
Watch out it's behind us!
Stop in the name of the law.
Evening all.
Raymond, come back! Why are you running away?

Then two men ran onto the stage....

followed by a policeman...   and a caretaker...

and a dragon.

Raymond said,

Where've you been, Ruby?
We've been waiting for you.
What took you so long?
Why are you always late?
Arrgh.
GRRH!!

Ruby replied,

Ruby chased Raymond around the stage.

GRRHH!
ARRGH!
ARRGH!
Eeek!!
GRRRH!
I could get to like this.
Ruby!
RUBY!
That's my girl.

The audience cheered. Ruby was the winner.

The curtains closed

It was the end of the play.

But it was not the end of the story.

Ruby Turner, come here.
Where were you? Why are you always late?
She made me look a fool, Miss.
Why did you kill Prince Raymond?
She broke my sword, Miss.
Now she's for it.
You ruined the play!!

But the Mayor was making a speech.

Ladies and gentlemen.
I have seen many school plays in my time, but that was the best I have ever seen.
What an original idea to have the dragon kill the Prince.
Who wrote the play?

Miss Williams stepped forward.

The Mayor gave her some flowers.

Oh...you shouldn't have!

Everybody cheered...

What a clever person you are.
Hooray!
Hooray!
Hooray!

...and cheered.

Miss Williams smiled.　The Mayor smiled.　The Headmaster smiled.

The policeman said,

One or two of the ideas came from Ruby.

Was Ruby the one dressed up as a dragon?

She stopped two burglars from stealing the money collected for charities. She saved the school cups!

Where is Ruby?

Ruby!
Ruby!
Ruby!

Ruby?

Ruby had gone.

Ruby was waiting for the bus.   She'd had enough of play-acting.

I think I'd rather be a pop-singer, anyway.

The bus conductor said,   said Ruby.

You're early.
Arrgh!

The bus took her home.

THE END.

First published in Great Britain by William Collins Sons & Co Ltd 1990

First published in Picture Lions 1991. Picture Lions is an imprint of the Children's Division,
part of HarperCollins Publishers Ltd, 77/85 Fulham Palace Road, Hammersmith, London W6 8JB

© text Gareth Owen 1990
© illustrations Bob Wilson 1990

Printed by Warners (Midlands) plc, Bourne + London